SHAKESPEARE IN SOHO

Jeremy Reed

SHAKESPEARE IN SOHO
Jeremy Reed's Remix of the Sonnets

 EYEWEAR PUBLISHING

First published in 2017
by Eyewear Publishing Ltd
Suite 333, 19-21 Crawford Street
Marylebone, London W1H 1PJ
United Kingdom

Cover design and typeset by Edwin Smet
Cover photograph by Getty Images, Hulton Archive
Author photograph by Gregory Hesse
Printed in England by TJ International Ltd, Padstow, Cornwall

ISBN 978-1-911335-22-1

*Eyewear wishes to thank Jonathan Wonham for his
generous patronage of our press.*

WWW.EYEWEARPUBLISHING.COM

JEREMY REED
is one of Britain's most
outstanding and famously controversial
poets, his originality of imagery and cutting
edge subject matter distinguishing him from
most of his contemporaries. His recent books
include the poetry collections *Piccadilly Bongo*,
Sooner Or Later Frank, *Voodoo Excess* and *Red
Light Blues*, as well as a biography of Lou Reed
Waiting For The Man and *The Dilly: A Secret
History of Piccadilly Rent Boys*. He wrote the
libretto for Marc Almond's 2015 album *Against
Nature*, and performs regularly in London and
Europe, both solo, and as one half of
The Ginger Light, a unique duo
combining performed spoken
word with electronics.

Note on the Poems

Shakespeare's sonnets really are a sequence, that falls into natural sections, in a progressive narrative peopled with memorable characters. The first 18 sonnets, for example, are exhortations to the character commonly known as the 'Young Man' to marry and beget children. This section ends with the lines 'So long lives this, and this gives life to thee', the story then becoming more personal and far, far more interesting. A painful, adoring series of addresses to the 'Young Man' are followed by the fascinating 'Dark Lady' section, and finally by oddly miscellaneous sonnets at the end. There are also several events which change the course of the story. For a few sonnets, our narrator becomes distracted by his all-consuming jealousy of a more successful poet; yet another section of the sequence is his reply to an unseen letter, and perhaps the most crucial moment in the journey of these sonnets is when the poet discovers that his mistress and his young man have betrayed him, with each other.

Jeremy Reed's sonnet series runs on parallel lines to Shakespeare's. His deep knowledge of Shakespeare is always evident in allusions to the latter's language, for example, imagery of the sun, rotting flowers, and the constant theme of impending old age. Some of Reed's sonnets are direct translations of Shakespeare's ('Do I compare thee to a peachy July day?', Reed's No. 8); many are entirely original; and some twist the sixteenth-century meaning altogether. For example, Shakespeare's Sonnet 7 'Lo! In the orient when the gracious light / Lifts up his burning head', ending pompously:

So thou thyself outgoing in thy noon
Unlooked on diest unless thou get a son.

is twisted in Reed's Sonnet 26, 'There's nobody isn't a
sun-watcher' which ends bitterly:

> So go get a wife
> as a means of validating your life.

Reading the two sonnets alongside each other,
comparatively, heightens the sarcasm of Reed's final
couplet. Yet it also makes us see that the solemn
admonishments to 'go forth and multiply' in
Shakespeare may not be entirely serious. In this way, the
suggested pairing of Reed's sonnets and Shakespeare's
in this book can enrich our understanding of what both
poets are doing.

Reed's 'remix' stands alone as a sonnet sequence and
story in itself, which is why we made the decision to
print it independently of Shakespeare's poems. The
two sonnet sequences do not mirror each other exactly.
However, reading even only the few of Shakespeare's
sonnets we have suggested alongside Reed's sonnets can
illuminate the language, technique and meaning of both
authors. We hope that as you become familiar with both
sets of sonnets, you will find this more and more.

Rosanna Hildyard
London, 2017

To The Only Begetter Of
These Living Sonnets

TOYOKO ITO

1 – *(See Shakespeare's Sonnet 20)*
A girl's face done by MAC in Harvey Nick's
is optimal focus, wide red liplines,
Studio Fix for finish and for kicks
a dusty silver eye-shadow that shines.
And guys, the ones who have a cooler look
attract by fashion and blue twinkling eyes –
I like a mixture of lowlife and crook
who upstage women by their bitchy lies
like Mr W H effortlessly
making them jealous, now I've named my man
you've got one on my sexuality
like a brand logo sloganning a can.
If he gets off with girls it ups the thrill
of what we do with a blue diamond pill.

•

2 – *(See Shakespeare's Sonnet 91)*
Some think position's all, or fat cat jobs,
or being on the rich list – fuck the lot,
hedge funders, celebs and real estate yobs,
arms dealers, bankers, they're like sugar rot.
I'd rather go for the ecstatic hit
of dopamine I get, Will, from your sort,
and even if our queer angles don't fit
society's, I'm glad you're an escort.
I'd rather have street trash than class,
and your 18-carat gold personality
than money markets – look: my refilled glass
shivers with how I feel, pure ecstasy.
But losing you, the thought's the bottom line
if I imagine you no longer mine.

3

It's hard to be a poet making out
from Southampton's estate and the next show
but living on the line juices up clout
sticky social networkers never know.
Wealth and honours oxidise, OBE
or Iron Cross, both soon disintegrate,
even Elvis bulked on obesity
and ballooned to the size of a sequinned gate.
Who remembers war criminals; Bush, Blair,
the Tudor quango? And my words shoot down
the evil that sexes up dossiers
or alligator queens who wear a crown.
I'd rather be nothing than everything;
a finger's lighter for not wearing a ring.

•

4

My dead friends live in me like astronauts
in zero gravity, dead lovers too
use up my oxygen as life support
their legacies leave me so bitter blue.
I don't do afterlife – if we survive
no friend's dropped by to talk of the party
in the white mansion where mirage men live,
I'd rather impact now, just you and me.
You've aspects of old lovers I let go,
we keep to types as cyclical routine,
can't break the habit – don't want you to know
I'd kill for jealousy if you weren't mine.
We're like Joe Orton and Ken Halliwell:
I know you're rent but, baby, do you sell?

5

Your ID's elusive like most rough trade
dissolving into the crowd, but I'm lost
in how you're special and mostly afraid
your 28" waist comes at a cost.
There's no-one got your look – drop-dead gorgeous,
in any bar, not dodgy like Kit Marlowe
dabbing foundation on his cuts like us
after we've fought watching my latest show.
Spring's here again, cherry blossom pompoms
ride on its curve and find you at your best
in summer too – I race through the seasons
my iPhone snapshots filling in the rest.
I see you everywhere – it's only me
revising visuals in my memory.

.

6

I'm self-consumed, there's no getting away
from my assumption there's no other star
that writes so effortlessly in this way.
I'm Ziggy Stardust taking it too far
the image as conceit – the me, me, me,
so inescapable I can't see round
the obstacle, focused identity,
with an intensity that bends my mind.
But when I check my face and see the lines
I break up inside, I can't get above
degrading age and how it undermines
youthful pretensions, so I can't believe
I'm anything to you, what use am I
except for cash in hand, living this lie?

7 – *(See Shakespeare's Sonnet 22)*
I've no conception of myself as old
except seeing you wasted on bad drugs
toxic chemicals sweating, you out cold
still paying off dealers and city thugs.
We're both the same – it's just my poetry
gives you the lift you don't appreciate
like flying business not economy
and both arriving in the same smashed state.
Watch out for yourself, like I do for you,
caring's a rarer sensitivity
we share or don't, and listen, baby blue,
we're windowed in the same reality.
We'd do it of course, a suicide pact,
and who dies first's a gratuitous fact.

•

8 – *(See Shakespeare's Sonnet 18)*
Do I compare you to a peachy July day,
only you're blonder, better energy,
and even if wind tore up most of May
your teen spirit promotes vitality.
The summer chokes, dusty air pollutants
contaminating gold light, CO_2,
fine particles, kerosene components,
the air in central London's hazy blue.
Youth's everything; say 19-30,
you don't think death, and loving you I try
to imagine you're post-biology
the only person who will never die.
Men size you up; you're sexy with street-cred,
the sort who in Soho turns every head.

9

Your look's so singular I'm fixed on it
like an addiction, it's almost a crime
and writing pushes it to the limit
my incurable obsession with time.
The mutual fear of ageing figures large
in both our lives. It eats you when you're gay.
Sugar daddy or escort, it's a charge
keeps us self-consciously aware all day.
Vulnerable, sensitive, beat up by life
we help our tribe; I keep a watch on you
and get hammered for ignoring my wife,
my STD an incurable do.
I use bath houses; one on Turnmill Street
raided by armed cops in the sticky heat.

•

10 – *(See Shakespeare's Sonnets 15-19)*
Nothing survives; we're de-branded designs,
dystopian, sad, death as the backstory
to all initiative, our frantic signs
fragile as impulses from a poppy.
Even Hitler's bunker and Blair's Fourth Reich
degrade: the tyrant in his corridor
sweating out fear. Summer gives us a hike,
a mood swing, roses tumbling at the door.
It's all too much – it's only love survives
like a jewel cut from an unfractured stone,
the rest is atomized like our messed lives
in which we ruthlessly end up alone.
I write by hand. You survive in black ink
Mr WH done in by drink.

11

When I Google our Earth I grow afraid
at devastation, a trembling moment
the best anything gets in our cosmic back yard
even the popping stars are small events.
We're flowers sprung by rain that come and go
under radioactive skies. Go find
a place that's safe – not even Mexico
offers refuge without losing your mind.
Young, we don't ever think we'll disappear.
Like Bob Dylan, still out there on the road
at vanishing point, and the fact we're queer
has ideas of heredity implode.
Whatever we lose with the years I try
to reverse by pretending you'll never die.

•

12

Passive acceptance, that's your character,
a sort of stoned optimal hedonist
stuck to a poet: you've no obvious war
with age or scratchy track marks on your wrist.
I see you standing on the highest stair
made-up, eyeliner pen shaping cat's eyes,
Nars powder dusting, blond streaks in your hair,
your emptiness like wide blue summer skies.
We do what we can to repair error,
(my theme's 154 remixes of age)
as though we lived in front of a mirror
with me carving you up for the big stage.
I use you for material – can it be
you have your own separate identity?

13

You've lost your mind, flipped into a psycho,
blank, delusional, and there's no one there.
It's drugs of course, and your hangers-on know
you've bitched on everyone and dyed your hair.
But if you've lost direction, try 'restart'.
In any Soho bar, you've got the looks
to sugar any sugar-daddy's heart
– like mine, except today no one reads books.
Why let your residual youth fade away?
At least married you'd have identity
against cold climate blues, a winter day
in which the dark's an end point come at 3.
You had a father, I'm the substitute
like pink paint dribbles splashed over a boot.

•

14

Youth's really got it, but it burns so fast
it's like hormonal rocket fuel, a rush
like dopamine, already it's the past
while living it as a full on car crash.
Its recollected beauty wins it back
the degradation of falling apart,
you make seventy like damaged train track
and still think twenty's the optimal part.
It's better to OD, exit before
dementia rots the brain with gunk, and look
get out before you crawl across the floor
like dead pop lacking an infectious hook.
Your mother never got from you a child
to do drugs, wreck a bedroom and run wild.

15

A pretty face – they're all in Selfridges –
ground floor for makeup and rose-pouty lips
the fashion floors you cross them like bridges
in every changing room there's someone strips.
You're just my type – I mean the sparkling eyes
burning out inside like a red quasar
and all the network of adhesive lies
with fast getaway like a Jaguar...
You're consumed by self-hate it makes you cruel,
you crowd the moment like a rhinestone ring,
petty, vicious, I'd never call you cool
but chilly like a white window in spring.
They come and go in life the good and bad.
I'm on the Menswear floor, so blue, so sad.

•

16

Youth starts at 40 and not middle age
and I project you there full of Botox,
no natural lesions and your entourage
partied out and, like you, slammed in detox.
Think back and further back, you won't regain
your fuck-off good looks, despite the rebuild,
or ever turn a sexed-up head again
outside Lloyds TSB still stoned on pills.
It's all too fast; our teens are so confused
we're never recognized for who we are:
exceptional. I look at you, you're used.
Already wasted like a fading star.
You need to keep back something that you've lost.
Winning and losing come at the same cost.

17

It's imperfection in a face attracts,
the damage-quotient, but you're obsessed
with re-makes, dressing up the look with facts,
Mac or No. 7. The way you're dressed,
your manner of giving nothing away
keeps you self-referential go-getter
so self-regarding facetiously gay,
biting your nails becomes a crowd-pleaser.
Self-consumed, self-interested, alone,
you chase reflections in the bar mirror
taking in nothing that's not on your phone
and hostile to each sexed-up predator.
Someone like you, you've never learnt to share
anything, but the angle of your hair.

•

18

You'd break a woman up and smash her heart
you're so committed to a fast burn-out,
no children – they're mundane – speeding's your art –
the casualty whose death's both gold and dirt.
The self-created individual star
they're best and have a sort of lucky gene
that's resistant to propping up the bar
and death's a wallop just like Jimmy Dean.
Look at your lifestyle; you've no self-esteem,
don't allow others in or care you'll die,
the most you've got for company's a clone,
you're so defensive there's no asking why.
You're self-destructive – it's just me, me, me
pops up first in every company.

19

You're scrambled by self-interest, so far gone
you're indifferent: it's the selfish gene
dominates like a junky – look you've done
your worst again: stamped on a spotty teen.
You're venomous with hate, it might be murder.
Self-harm in bathrooms, did it to yourself
in the Ritz bar and glitzy Dorchester
smashed all the bottles on a mirrored shelf.
Clean up your act and I'll help you rehab
at the Priory, give you another chance.
Like killing bacteria off in the lab,
your tantrums killed off my last squeezed advance.
Do it, peel off the layers and get back
to who you were, like playing the right lick.

•

20

A planet-hunter, I sprinkle stardust
into your luck, the stars burn energies
as exoplanets like limo exhaust
plumed red and blue, hot toxicities.
If war and murder's just a shot away
and planetary meltdown full in the face
we're ready to lift-off, you go your way
I'll take the faster climb out into space.
Looking at you I learn the bigger end
from little habits, stars crunched to a grain
and all that shit about being your friend
it's like Tate & Lyle sugar rots the brain.
I'd wish you of course to be a billionaire.
Rob city banks – one way of getting there.

21

The better years in which you got it right
less aggro and more equanimity
crashed like ditching a car back of the night
or crashing the same car twice, ref: Bowie.
You can't catch summer and its lazy pop,
winter strips most things bare, like stamped-on feet,
and has you dream of a planetary hop
instead of busking on the stone-cold street.
Summer's like a gold brushstroke: remember
the raised glass of Sauvignon Blanc filmed it
a moment – purple heat trapped in thunder
and what we value most we soon forget.
I live by that: the flowers we cut were great,
most chances in life come too soon or late.

·

22

Obsessed with looks I don't want you to change
but remain fixed 20 – 30 most.
A pretty boy whose art's to re-arrange
the same style: who would want you if it's lost?
There's one iconic image gets you right
the Gold and Spice in Dubai, casual shot,
and if you got ten kids on ten club nights
you'd be no happier; and it's a threat
you'll do it, clone yourself through IVF
like Michael Jackson's intra-species gene,
simply to outlive what you can't address
the wear and tear you don't get as a teen.
The choice is yours, cryonics or the flash
of being burnt and atomized to ash.

23
Born April 23 1564
Died April 23 1616
Aged 52
This likeness taken 1603
Age at that time 39 years
the assumed portrait. Music's mostly pop
and its derivatives: Ziggy appears
as red-haired android making a time-hop
faster than any of my characters.
The riff's like altered state – a brain reward
sensitising dopamine receptors,
right-brain fritzes: it stops me in a yard.
Rock's about sex: go find someone and fuck.
To be alone accelerates bad luck.

•

24 – *(See Shakespeare's Sonnet 3)*
I keep reminding you to check your face,
do something with it, pull up fashion tips,
go to Harvey Nicks or travel deep space
to reverse time; but keep those bee-stung lips.
There's no one needs to age, get a nose job
at the Harley Street Clinic; but it's me
seeing myself in you who'd like the jab
to sugar up my acute jealousy.
You look like your mother at twenty-one
in a glossed hatch-back and reflective shades
head angled left and staring at the sun
like the edit before the music fades.
We're both obsessed by death and where we go
after it happens – read the sign FOLLOW.

25

I'm Will and in love with Will, there isn't time
to do Emilia. The violet sky
gives way to night: same-sex isn't a crime.
Night deepens. The tree outside's slow to die,
its dead leaves skitter in surges, a red
persists like red lipliner, and the park's
a shot-down entropy, most things are dead,
men hang out in the bushes early dark.
A beauty-junky, you're my fantasy
eroticised by recall: stay the same
don't go changing ever – I'm addicted, see,
to this intense dissociative game.
Stay single in our triangle – I feed
on you in my mind every single need.

•

26 – *(See Shakespeare's Sonnet 7)*

There's nobody isn't a sun-watcher
5 billion tonnes of helium burn per second
at its eruptive core. The Mars Rover's
so compact you can visualise its mind.
Follow the sun; most people do its curve
and couldn't we trade winter for its heat
at Grand Canaria, like we deserve
to live for ever in its gold heartbeat.
It's all over so fast: the seatback trays
fastened for landing- a foggy Heathrow
replaces what we had – sun-dazzled days –
with grey soapy weather out the window.
Don't want to do it? So go get a wife
as a means of validating your life.

27

You don't believe a single word I write,
why should you? – lying's central to my art
like doing drugs, I'll never get it right
and so the reader only gets a part.
And even if I used a Pantone chart
to match your eyes, they're turquoise, sometimes green,
some motherfucker would get a quick start
by saying the right colour's in between.
Most writing fades like a graffiti slash,
given 5 years the construct's out of date
the expression dirty as laundered cash
the meaning like a train arriving late.
But you'll live on in it like dated pop
as my revenge, despite your pleading *stop*.

•

28

My writing's visual, it's like video,
I colour you up like it was Reece Mews,
Bacon working from a paint-slashed photo
in a textured assault of pinks and blues.
Sometimes I get it right the morph I need
the underlying riff I find in you.
I don't waste time, accelerated speed's
my way of writing controversial new.
It's all done through transmission – eye to hand
the sun's part of the mix, I need the light
to help locate the things I understand
and get your Vitamin B levels right.
Seeing's not feeling, there's a conscious split.
When reconstructing you, the two don't fit.

29
My eye and heart in conflict, ain't it war
and that you're Will increases the conflict
as though seeing myself drunk at the bar
I'm seeing you like I couldn't predict.
We've been so secret my wife doesn't know
I picked you up at Shoreditch and obsessed
tried to become you – we're in one window
of shot emotions: same-sex and same-dressed.
Even a quick fling's complex, straight or gay,
we morph a face or body to create
the one we'd like to fuck and go away
pretending, searching for an online date.
My eye looks over you, sometimes my heart,
you should have known it from the very start.

•

30
The same old issues leave emotional scars
like faulty track: what do I do with you
or anyone, my mind lives in the stars.
My friend Kit Marlowe beat you black and blue.
I keep your photo on my phone and fix
on its erotics, sometimes on your face
and base pair by base pair your double helix
fascinates, like a new planet in space.
I can't get free of you in my crammed mind's
hyped-up neural pathways, and win or lose
we're really rude-boys, just two of a kind
and our contentiousness is what I choose.
But falling asleep I rotate our lives
like a tumble-dryer, see what survives.

31

I'm sugar daddy to your love of bling
in Harrod's monumental mortuary
and just the thought of you is everything
in and out of a crashed economy.
I keep debating if we're best alone
or on the scene hanging out in Soho
and being older I'm the awkward one
while you drink the bar under and I go
to Bar Italia. I make demands
or I'm too casual, never natural,
I'm all-or-nothing, fielding your commands,
or wanting to have you against a wall.
I've never learnt to compromise, I'm hot
or cold, both get too little or the lot.

•

32

Lou Reed's the one, 'I'm Waiting for the Man',
like me Southampton, grab your loot, don't gloat
over the contents, catch me if you can,
I'd say Will No. 2 you've missed the boat.
Dinners don't mean much: it's the company
I pick at like jewels from a smash-and-grab,
and rough trade stimulates acrimony
in the Ritz dining room, munching a slab
of boar, but we've the look, customized shirts,
bespoke jackets, I mean those buckskin boots
the Stones at sixty wear, and little hurts
accumulate, we've all been male escorts.
Try keep impartial. Dilly boys are best.
Southampton had some and I got the rest.

33

I was so careful, bought up real estate,
grabbed money for my plays as cash in hand,
and nurtured you through every shattered state
and even wrote bubblegum for our band.
You gave it all away, love and money,
trashed what we shared, broke me up like a chair,
and if you beat me I'd still think, honey,
of nothing but the highlights in your hair.
I gave you freedom, stayed invisible
at times you needed unconditionally,
fisted out cash wads over the table
and kept you lived up in my memory.
I'll lose you like the rest, of course. The hurt
comes from extracting a diamond from dirt.

•

34

It's like that, life gets harder every day,
DNA error, wear and tear, tax loss,
hammered emotions: when you come and stay
I talk money like giving a car gloss.
The war in me – I'm bi but take it on,
and if it's problematic I'm best gay
but confusing, my testosterone
peaks with you, babe. I have my special way.
If I'm on self-destruct then it hurts bad
the reprimands I give myself and the booze,
I round on the pub's arena, it's sad,
I'm 91 per cent star stuff but choose
to think the best's behind, the worst ahead
and that anyhow I'm better by far dead.

35

Relationships deteriorate so fast
they're scrambled shambles: I go underground
to the country: my wife thinks you're the past
but we rebuild, always the wrong way round.
I took it fast, was I dosed up on speed
the whole time as a transformative tool
thinking you were the only one – my need
disproportionate to your sexy cool?
I'm always rushed just like the Central Line,
it's once and once only the chance comes up
with this intensity. I'm yours you're mine,
the dance music we hear won't ever stop.
You know the song 'Love Will Tear Us Apart' –
it themed our disruptive moods from the start.

•

36

If I could teleport myself into
parallel processing, overtake time
I'd use it as spook surveillance on you
weaponized telepathy as invasive crime.
Marriage keeps me provincial, energy's
a wave form – I don't need to be one place
but quantum, simultaneous reality,
like someone exiting time into space.
If I could become *thought* not *projection*,
the *poem* not the *poet*, hijack you
into a sort of alien abduction
I'd code the secret in these lines as clues.
It breaks me up, the physical's so slow,
even its green light don't seem to say go.

37

Do the right drug, you enhance empathy,
you're air and fire, from Limehouse to Shoreditch
I zap you with zingy telepathy,
we're on and off, but I still need you, bitch,
in short doses, tenderness doesn't last
a single meeting – I'm obsessed with death
and all the mad scenes attached to my past
and you slaloming on crystal meth.
I miss you, rapid-firing impulses
into your brain, untraceably in disconnect,
as though your hexagonal molecules
are the only gene coding I select.
Can't live with or without you, stay or go
I've no idea – I say yes, mean no.

•

38 – *(See Shakespeare's Sonnet 27)*
Sleepless again, I'm too wired up to rest,
body done in, but saturated mind
shooting disruptive movies, do my best
to shut brain-chatter in the blanks I find.
I recreate the things we say and do
only they're altered and manipulate
reality – I don't know which is true
like men hanging around the subway gate.
You fascinate like a moody ruby,
a black jewel living in me half the night
like garnet LEDS and in weak gravity
float like a Starman in and out of sight.
It makes me hard, anticipating sex –
two bodies thrashing round in a vortex.

39
I stare at you incessantly, it's sick,
(I had Chris Beeston back of Bishopsgate)
and even though you're just another trick
my feelings split an apple, love and hate.
You're light and dark, upbeat and moody blue
and I'm attracted to your darker side
the underground character shining through
like a punctured can nudged in by the tide.
Can't take my eyes off you, like Wriothesley
dragged up, the patron who gets off on you.
You're my explosive sexual fantasy
awake, asleep and in between the two.
My days and nights dissolve so seamlessly
they're interchangeable like you and me.

•

40 – (*See Shakespeare's Sonnet 27*)
I reach for sleepers, else I'm up all night,
red eyes hallucinating all the mess
come up between us, and with you it's right
that booze and hypertension up my stress.
You're so contagious you invade my sleep
tweaking my double life, probing my shame,
I live with it, driving a blacked-out jeep.
Your jealousy's bacterial to this game.
I blow things out of proportion, admit
it's me exaggerates the way you spook
my insecurity, just look at it,
my madness keeps repeating like a hook.
We track each other, losing you or not
I realise you're everything I've got.

41

I can't de-stress to make it through the night
manically hyper heading for the drop.
It's only the alteration of light
informs my burnt out system when to stop.
There's rest in neither, you're my boy poison
like venom in a vein, but I still write
as compulsive feedback loop, so switched-on
I do it giving words a sensual bite.
But you, you're out there in the big green day
picking a bar, the foggy river's slide
slapping wharves, the moment's yours today
while I grow moody sitting by the tide.
I'm at the bottom, it's like a black pit
this abject serotonin deficit.

•

42 – (See Shakespeare's Sonnet 73)
Autumn's my season, stringy yellow leaves
resisting, shivering on the road
or wind trashed trees extending red-gold leaves
over a dirt path patterned like a toad.
In me you sense a death-bound gravity,
a used-up, lived-in, waiting-for-the-end,
syphilitic flare-up; yes even me
I'll disappear too, round an orbital bend.
Not Alzheimer's, Aids, just hammered by
persistent stress, wear and tear of a wife
who doesn't tolerate my sodomy.
The more I have of it, the worse my life.
The thought of leaving you's what I can't take,
like throwing this book into a black lake.

43 — *(See Shakespeare's Sonnet 19)*
You'll be the death of me and me of you,
but something in these lines will hang around
as residue and be picked up as new
as bits and pieces accidentally found.
It's only words printed by Thomas Thorpe,
but rub them and you have my DNA
and writing's like a time-slip, a time-loop
in which traces of you can't get away.
And when I'm dead you'll play an indie song
that makes you sad and I'll have lost the gift
to reconstruct you in words. It's all wrong
we die off like interplanetary drift.
The worth of anything's a short-term thing
like romance colouring this sordid fling.

•

44
Rephrase it, me writing your epitaph,
you dead from Aids or viral pandemic
our fragmented despairing personal loss
commonplace, transformed by verbal magic.
I'd like your name to live, mine disappear,
perversely self-destructive I won't know
about my legacy, that's very clear,
I sing it also: 'Baby please don't go.'
The Earth's a wobbly devastated cone,
some future readers may connect and feel
our same-sex affair now it's come and gone
shone like an emerald when it was real.
Take it or leave it, as if you could care.
I rip up convention like few would dare.

45
It's disappointment breaks me up again,
death's in the feedback loop as obsession,
not as an opposite but equal pain
a sort of arbitrary repossession,
what do you want of it – the whole lot gone
and this and that and this and that and that,
no free speech, the poetry police moved in
(Armitage, Motion) or some fucked up twat
with their minus zero imagination.
Death's a grey interzone like Warren Street,
a state like living in the wrong nation,
all pleasures gone, even the right to tweet.
I'd lose the lot: it's you I can't pretend
makes what we've got impossible to end.

•

46
Just go and party on the day I die.
I've chosen to be slammed into dug earth
for slow decay – but I'm hoping to fly
into subtle processes of rebirth.
You might remember what my hand has done
shaping imagery like re-entry flare
into poetry, I'm the only one
who shot through red lights as a scary dare.
Read something of mine for magic or luck
and celebrate our sharing good and bad
together, like house paint dribbles stuck
on a Mink Dulux can. Go out, be mad,
distract yourself; grieving won't restore me
except as wave-patterns, a frequency.

47 – (See *Shakespeare's Sonnet 32*)
If you outlive me, Will, the survivor
of everything we knew, do better things
than hang on to my repeated error
of poetry, like a fist of dead rings.
Only a partner keeps those things alive,
books come and go like brand initiatives
trashed as ephemera, the more you live
the less anything but hedge fund survives.
I'd rather you celebrate life not art
my reckless organic chutzpah, the dope
I smoked as Virginia Black, there's the smart
I've cranked up: other writers try their scope.
Love me so fiercely, I'll feel it when dead
the shattered motion of a rocky bed.

•

48
Death's particle X in the pineal gland,
a gene code default – don't come back to bars
we signatured, go form an indie band,
I'll write you poems in the dusty stars.
But you can do PR on the sonnets
propagate their juiced mix as Shoreditch cult
documenting same-sex like red sunsets
flaming with CO_2 and the occult.
You're stuck with my dodgy controversy
like carbon footprints, dissociate from my name
or you'll alienate edgy family
by associating with toxic fame.
Our love's a dead end, now we're known as queer
move into a new quarter and go clear.

49

I need rapid firing neuronal drive
to activate resources I can't find
as sparky facility, poems live
like streaming video into the mind.
Age don't mean nothing, but I'm hung on it,
and you Will, remind me of what I've lost,
age is the desert boot that never fits
the wearer, look the damage comes at cost.
I try to get you in the poem's frame
as if you care to focus, you've no choice
my bandit kleptomania gets you fame,
it's my pathology – poetic voice.
You know your worth – I'll never get it right
and if I did there'd be a vicious fight.

•

50

You've got no rival, unilaterally
a poem goes one way, you can't contest
mixed up emotions, control freakery
I put in what I like and pull the rest.
Poems don't earn, they're more like condom lube
the surface gloss – I don't always get you
but squeeze your character out of a tube
and hope you find in yourself something new.
Style over content, that's my happy hour
extravaganza, I distort you hun,
glitzing up metaphorical firepower
and making you into the only one.
Writing about you's selfishly the art
of demeaning and ripping you apart.

51

Base pair by base pair I build poetry
as double helix, get your name out there
as coded. In the Mermaid pub we're free
to hitch you to my lines, as if I care
Ben Jonson overhears: he killed a man,
while it's my thoughts I value, not their flash
conversion into words, like astrakhan
thrown on the shoulders to emphasize cash.
I bought the gatehouse at Blackfriars, a deal
dodgier than our item – you don't need
my image-squirts, better to go get real,
pitch as a rent boy. Can you even read?
There's others respect speech I write on down
as books are a cult in our part of town.

•

52

It's mania to devote this space to you
154 sonnets as delusional
commentary singularly my point of view
like photo-shooting you against a wall
5,000 times. It's a gateway to early death
to be inspired by someone dangerous
so that your molecules stream on my breath
like a cloned necrophiliac fetish.
It's always like this babe, dichotomy
between virtual and real – I think you're mine
but you float round me in weak gravity
like attempting to fuck you on the line.
I substitute words for you, like a spook
throwing figures to imitate your look.

53

I've got you under my skin like venom
knowing I'm just the intermediary
hotting you up, insidious poison
I call spontaneous telepathy.
Your fame's already out – it's like a boat
kids stone in a Thames pool, a paper sail
I've written on, the thing can hardly float
like my low self-esteem and how I fail
to match my rivals – I'm your second choice
to a new pick-up – Liberty wallet,
Coutts account, younger and burning more juice,
I'm dissed out and vicious with slow-burn regret.
And if I lose you I've myself to blame
for being inadequate to the game.

•

54

A poem is no substitute for sex,
I used you up in words – you needed cock
and crashed into an emotional vortex
and now even my lines have lost their shock.
You're kind about it; sugar-daddies fade
and end up kicking cans along the quay
as bitter outlaws. Mostly I'm afraid
I robbed you of your look for poetry.
Your boyfriend's symbiotically inclined
to take shine from you; it's a part exchange
in which each helps the other be refined
without too much effort in personal change.
He'll pay for you assuming it's himself
he's purchasing, and ends up on the shelf.

55 – *(See Shakespeare's Sonnet 55)*
I go for glam androgynous beauty
as inspiration – and don't know its source
this variable orbital frequency
with you the cute recipient of course.
I'd argue your good looks the paradigm
of butch I have to colour to do right
and it's an abstract no-colour you gain
by my mixing inner and outer sight.
Why bother, can't I just accept your face
without the need to recreate a look
that's 'really' you? – I'm thinking of the space
you'll later occupy inside a book.
It's schizo, wanting to keep you a teen
as somebody the reader's never seen.

•

56
You needed Francis Bacon explode paint
to rough you to visual autopsy
not my attempts to make you same-sex saint
and time-slip you out of your century.
I've backgrounded myself in this report
like sleeping intermittently on long haul
this modern affair with a male escort
living back of a media scandal.
We've been so confidentially discreet,
I gave you words, kept you out of trouble,
our double life always so incomplete
we kept it concealed in a pink bubble.
There's so much about you I'll never know
atomized like a dispersing rainbow.

57
I'd commit crimes for you, insanity's
a part of it, remember what we did
in the Rose Theatre loft? I can't, you see,
break out of this electrifying grid.
I treat you good most times; write up today
like it's tomorrow, that's one way to love,
the present as the future – look that way
the indicator board points time to leave.
I boast truth, honesty and kindness, three
aspects that fit with caring, do they fit
with what you want, twisted perversity
from a sugar cool rock'n'roll bandit?
There's no assurance things will work, let's try
to give it one more go to reach the sky.

•

58
'You go to my head' it's Billie Holiday
reinventing my whooshed-up incentive
to iconize you in this hyped-up way
hoping we'll wormhole through time and survive.
It's so invasive, slicing up your mind
like deli salami, your voice ain't heard
and I'm full-on subjective, what I find
don't dust you up with a cyanide word.
You're an inspirer, a Pop Tart poet
by what you give, avoidance of the old
and all that boring stuff in the remit
of Larkin without molecular gold.
The kicks I get from writing turn to pain
best heard in Robert Johnson's 'Love In Vain'.

59

I've used you up so often like a car
ditched by the road, hijacked you like a clone
for subject matter as a fallen star
half the bar has your picture on their phone.
Your street-blue eyes are cyan head-turners
even a hoodie wouldn't bash your face
one flutter of those sexy slow-burners
hormones burn like a rocket into space.
Your share in this it's always second-hand
and means nothing unless you read the stuff
and when I raise the level you can't stand
the fact I elevate what's rude and tough.
I'm not better than you; we're the same kind
only I reconstruct you in my mind.

.

60

Tom Ford's Crimson Noir as a red lipline
sometimes I get a girl and you don't know
at the George Inn and I don't call her mine
she's the dark end of a brothel's rainbow.
The moon's regolith and the sun's burn-out,
their energies connect with what we do,
like the sea's undercover jewels that hit
the hissing shore in variants of blue.
I'd like to set the record accurate
no-one compares to you, and if it's sad
I keep you secret, then it's far too late
to decode WH and too bad
I can't sell out – we'd hang for what we risk,
the rumour alone like a verbal frisk.

61

I substitute words for reality
and you're occupied by touch-devices,
it's delusional hallucinatory
to glamourize our underworld vices.
You could do better – Ritz tea with a hedge funder,
weaponizing your mind, not your body,
just being you without the reminder
I'm a spy code-breaking your privacy.
One thing you won't better's my poetry,
I've got the measure of you and it's done
like downloaded genes your biography
I've fictionalised into the only one.
I've got your number; others get it wrong,
I'm sure you'd rather be in a pop song.

•

62 – *(See Shakespeare's Sonnet 67, 68)*
He's at the STD clinic today.
We're both infected. Viral weaponry
is complementary to being gay
a combative gene with society.
If he's in makeup, men do it better,
you'd think his lips a full-on summer rose
that pouty, a subversion of gender
right to the beauty spot left of the nose.
Straight poets lack the dimension of bi,
and if he died I'd lose the only one,
like Bowie's 'one in a million' I try
to keep him feminine and girlie thin.
He's modern like the present that we see
in the rear-view mirror as history.

63
Never too busy to be beautiful,
glamour needs show, a Japanese stylist
like a rose scent, so its red potential
brims like a pout above a thorny fist.
Decay's as richly vermilion as bloom,
a deeper bruise-red fascinates by blue
inclusions, like their die-off in a room,
twelve dead roses reminding me of you
and your erotic youth brings into play
as seminally explosive – it's so fast
sex and roses, they're both over today
like the optimal present's in the past.
And you Will, faded like denim, I try
to fool myself baby you'll never die.

·

64
Bobby Brown, Space NLC, YSL,
I like the lot for the dusty rainbow
makeup projects and for its overkill
on men, semi-matte reds shaped as a bow.
Feed on controversy, Emilia, Will,
as my sex gang, a black and a white skin,
and if we're subterraneans, a pill
or drink will keep our notoriety in.
Emilia, you've reached a platform where years
have levelled out like standing in your heels
the way sometimes a second youth appears
and its apparent in the way it feels
in you as acceptance, go do it, wear
a push-up D-cup bra, and redo your hair.

65 – *(See Shakespeare's Sonnets 69, 70)*
Your look gets deconstructed on the street
the way you walk and dress gets pulled apart
by the contentiously hostile you meet
looking for rebuild, rehab or restart.
I don't know how you do it; keep your cool
from every angle, chilling Soho Square,
inner and outer breaking every rule
and Converse All Star part of getting there.
They can't see the gold honey in your mind
open like a yellow chrysanthemum
but vilify what good in you they find
like Blair's thrill – depleted uranium.
You'll always get above it, all that trash
their signature like fingerprints on cash.

•

66
Just do your worst by walking out on me,
I'd like a civil partnership; you're not
that kind, but my dependency
means that I've always got to have you hot.
I get the rumour you see other guys
and try to do my own thing, but I'm sold
on you distractively, no matter tries
to liberate my attraction to gold.
And now you've rocked me to insanity,
stressed me out I've started to find myself,
so watch out honey, there's no certainty
I won't come back at you by dodgy stealth.
You're cheating, two-timing, and don't pretend
you'll ever change or our confusion end.

67

I'm your sex-slave and crawl across the floor
to pleasure you, I blame myself for this
optimal sauna heat, you still want more,
the lip bruises rubbed in with every kiss.
When we're apart I imagine the lot
intensified as solitary pleasure,
like a ruby worn on the skin gets hot
I recreate what we do at leisure.
You're my instructor, a strange attractor,
we've ruined each other's lives, but why stop,
we're watched in bars by sniffy undercover
and getting away's like a planet-hop.
If you keep distant, then I'm hotter still
anonymous high-octane energy Will.

•

68

I always side with you when you attack
my vulnerability, say 'right, what's wrong?'
I'm often your mean singer dressed in black
lip-syncing the B-side of a hit song.
It's my anthologised faults you expose,
my shocking masochism that admits
to things you've done as mine, and always those
corrupt patterns grown into weird habits.
It's such a messy self-destructive scene
the way I take your abuse like a drug
telling you what I've done and where I've been
and turning you into a druggy thug.
I soak up all your hatred; get my kicks
from you and other street toughs, other tricks.

69

Don't leave me for my faults because they hurt
me worse than you, I won't retaliate
at accusations or rip off your shirt
or ever turn on you juiced up by hate
throwing my anger at you like a glass
exploded on the wall – I've no comeback
at your emotional punches, I can't pass
on your undercover insider's track.
Go missing from our Soho walks, you'll find
news of me from your friends, it can't be hid
the space you take up, bigger than my mind
hallucinating you all over this grid.
I soak up your abuse; I'm up to here
with the confused discourse of being queer.

•

70

Abject, humiliated, I despise
the way I crawl to you and feed you sex,
give up my writing, desperately reprise
the same compromises – bad juju hex
in which I threaten the world ends if you
walk out on me, dystopian apocalypse
like 9/11 instructing my blue-
mooded tantrums if I don't get your lips.
I don't know who you're with or where you are
only my jealousy distorts gossip,
you're in the backroom of a Vauxhall bar
doing a raunchy hammered burlesque strip.
I take the lot coz I can't let you go
and sniff your trail out all over Soho.

71

So I'll keep up the illusion you're mine
like a rejected husband and pretend
we're still an item, though you treat me mean
and I invent tricks to defer the end.
You conceal motives like a neat store thief,
impassive features, there's no give away,
you've lifted everything but my belief
in accepting what I've lost anyway.
You're sweet as *tarte au citron*, but you're hard,
the sticky superficiality
a donut's sugar dusting, in Ham Yard
you threatened me with public indecency.
You've looks, but they're like casino dice
thrown as an edgy get lucky quick vice.

•

72

So many mornings I've seen golden light
scattered with carbon check in from the sun
as fine particle chemistry, I'm right
the light's more beautiful for pollution.
The cloudbase purples over Southwark Bridge
the city's aorta churning finance,
but for this sunny moment on a ledge
beside the river, I, on impulse, dance
in shimmying photons atomized gold,
over industrial fixtures, office towers,
and in the surging moment don't feel old
or lacking in sexy hormonal powers,
and you Will, you're in the rush hour down there
in the tube crunching ozone-whiffy air.

73 – *(See Shakespeare's Sonnet 34)*
You promised everything that July day
significantly slashed by dazzling rain
and jacketless I seemed to run away
not from the driving downpour, but my pain.
I licked it home, my shirt steamed to my back
the thrashed torrential shattering downpour
scaring up shock: you stood there on attack,
no towel to hand, water puddling the floor.
You showed no shame, only perverse contempt,
re-treading old rows, rebuilding disgrace
you'd brought on me, as though you were exempt
from the offence and bruises on my face.
I took a shower and cried: you couldn't care,
threatening more pills, while redoing your hair.

•

74
I lost her for you, not a Shoreditch bitch,
but Emilia, gone with a financier,
the clout of rejection whacks this last ditch
city's poet, her greased city slicker
Canary Wharf trader facing me down,
his sleazy sneer at seeing me cut up
pulled like a handgun. You're cruising in town,
and fuelled by Cialis he never stops.
And you: you've had her too, I'll lose the lot
if you go threesome, triangular sex,
and me scrambled, deserving what I got
inside this confused turbulent vortex.
If you're my friend, I'll take the other loss
and send you carjack his cellulose gloss.

75 – *(See Shakespeare's Sonnet 36)*
Take half of me, the loves I've ever had
as accumulative debris and go,
saturated in rent you'll go half-mad
with all that loopy screwed-up undertow.
Grab every memory like a biker heist
smashing a window, you won't get inside
the secret lawless code that I resist
telling, like bankers I've so much to hide,
my laundered ID – poets don't get rich,
but you persist, turning me inside out
to locate damage and you'll never hitch
blackmail to finding what I'm all about.
But I can't hate you; all I've got's my life,
the force you threaten sometimes with a knife.

•

76
You're only happy digging dirt on me,
shattering me like a red rose smashed by rain
and what explodes is your duplicity
washing your own police record down the drain.
We're locked in conflict spiked by mutual guilt
discrediting each other's lives, look man,
you'd take me out, and I'd come back to squirt
venom on Twitter, like a red spray can.
You're rough trade and belong to a brothel
where men don't care providing they get off
on mechanical fantasies you sell
like trading on a virtuoso riff.
You're jaded, without edge, and soon you'll be
a loser, like most pick-up casualties.

77

Part of it's inequality, your teen spirit,
my retro-caution – how can we get on,
your faults are natural, why should you commit
to anything but wild revolution?
You're like a queen flashing a rhinestone ring,
some bit of glitzy paste, crystal sparkler,
but lack of taste in youth is everything,
don't bother me – if you're a carrier
I couldn't care – obstreperous wild child
acting the wolf – a black wolf at Blackfriars
taken up with the song 'Born To Be Wild',
morals like honours belong to cheap liars.
I like you any way you are: stone, mad
and pointing a gold finger at being bad.

•

78 – *(See Shakespeare's Sonnet 35)*
Don't regret anything, there isn't time,
roses are spiky, fountains silver mud,
good's often integrated into crime,
clean genes are mixed with error in your blood.
Even I fuck up when writing out our lives.
Authorising what's queer, just risk the lot's
the only way our chance story survives,
I'm in it with you what we've done and got.
I rationalise my sensual overload
to no affect, we're partners working through
our take on life on the same torn up road,
doing things that we always knew we'd do.
I'm an accessory to you, sweet thief,
and, even though I've got one, you're my wife.

79
Your petty crimes liberate you into
a rebellious freedom uncensored by
the check I keep, unconscious overview
of misdemeanours which elude my eye.
You're cool to look at baby; it's an art
(Emilia), you can't be won and I
prefer Will anyway. With you *restart*,
is always so perverse I want to die.
You'd break my heart like splitting an orange,
your beauty on/off thing, no longer sure
of instant pulls and I don't think it strange
you play with me to pretend a future.
You two-time me, hurting yourself and him
and Will's dilemmas like Lou Reed's 'Oh Jim'.

•

80
It's always winter when we separate,
December blues, I know it in my heart,
twenty minus zero, and I'm too late
to rehabilitate our sexy start.
We didn't count the summer, October's
spectacular leaf fall all red and gold
was like crushing a fig, I remember
café meetings before the increasing cold
killed energies. Remember the gold haze
we floated through like mirage men, now slashed
by seasonal change and alcoholic daze?
Our walks leaf-littered, where a jay once flashed
a turquoise splash, the trees are stripped-back nude
and together each powers-up solitude.

81

Let's try again, make a new start, re-tread
euphoric attraction that's lost its bite,
attempt to fire-up what's already dead
like a foggy opal catching the light.
There's nothing left, dishonesty's the sham
we substitute and boredom interferes
most times we meet, it weighs less than a gram
but always insidiously reappears.
We're like the choppy Thames' tidal fall,
submerged debris revealed after the tide
retreats, petrol drums banged against the wall
and both, exposed have everything to hide
that's kept covered. Winter's a hard one,
it makes us long to strip off in hot sun.

•

82 – *(See Shakespeare's Sonnet 98)*
I've been away all spring – check my passport,
cherry and almond blossom surfing froth –
and I'm depressed you're again an escort,
the season unrolled like a bolt of cloth.
Nothing recharges me, no whiffy scent
alerts my senses to magnolia flowers,
or the blue iris as purple event
or shattered excitement of April showers.
I didn't see the lily's effusion
or vermilion pigment heightening the rose,
their figures soaked into my confusion
the poems that I wrote you read like prose.
You seemed still full of winter SAD
driving me up and down the wall, half-mad.

83

I'm not demanding, if you hear me out,
nor less intense when holding feelings back
I'd rather keep secret what we're about.
(Gossip comes through distorted and off-track.)
Our fling was episodic, mostly spring,
exuberant euphoria one day,
depression next, we thought summer would bring
an orange Sunday not a blue Monday.
August turned bad; our storms were like the rain,
our run-ins predicting we'd go under,
emotional riot recreating pain
and in the city explosive thunder.
I'll tell you nothing; you've heard it in pop,
how rowing aggro's the hardest to stop.

•

84 – *(See Shakespeare's Sonnets 81–85)*
Don't want to write about it but forget
and yet poetry fine-tunes every scene
exhausting nerves, so my worst mood's re-set
in trying to pretend I'm still a teen.
I'd access inspiration from the stars
to fire-up processing, but words go dead
so often, me lazing the day in bars,
I need my gift startle traffic-light red.
Go, do! is what I tell myself: don't wait,
time's integrated into speed of light
and if I grab it, some other fucker's too late
to get the same thought-pattern come out right.
I'd give you fame, but can't prevent your death;
words sparkle like diamond-dust on my breath.

85

I see you future-forward wrecked like me,
wasted, crushed, damaged and dysfunctional,
your facial lines leathered injuriously
like Keith Richards: the writing's on the wall
and you don't care, your blood tests come back bad,
your liver's fatty, you're degenerate.
And even now you're prematurely sad
and not an option for a casual date.
I'm stuck with you – you look a runaway
signatured by junk food, opportune theft,
but you're the one I chose, it goes that way,
degradation until there's nothing left.
You'll live by what I wrote – I've got you fixed
as Mr WH I've remixed.

•

86 – (*See Shakespeare's Sonnet 81*)

Time zaps the lot. Even a lion's paws
lose combative swipe, big cats end up skins,
testosterone burns out, cells turn outlaws,
the mini-skirted girl loses her pins.
It's good and bad, can't ever win, the hurt
in losing youth can't be repaired, one year
you're twenty, the next forty and alert
to how there's no face doesn't disappear.
I keep on asking there's one person spared
slow ruin of his looks? Of course, it's him:
my bit of rough, and everything we've shared
left like a lipstick mark caked on a rim.
If words mean anything, someone somewhere
might read this and connect with my despair.

87

His face I knew, mapped now by city wear,
and I'm to blame for his despondency
at losing looks, he's hunted and aware
youth's blown, petals sliced off like a poppy.
His blond hair – will it still grow in the grave?
I run against the thought like a blank wall,
as though there really isn't much to save
from his biological funeral.
He's like a summer snapshot that won't change
as mental image, a one-off that hurts,
can't recreate *him* next July, it's strange
how individual pick-ups stay alert
to a prototype, keep your looks modern,
and attitude – there's not much left to learn.

•

88

The way I see you you'll never grow old
internally – 3 years, that's what we've shared,
3 summers conceding to autumnal gold,
we're close as a double helix is paired.
3 effusive springs in your company,
April's drenched perfume levelled out by June,
and still our first meeting pops magically
into the moment – a guitar in tune.
But it's illusion, time stands still; it moves
inside our blood, atomized, corrosive,
and his soft complexion's patterned with grooves,
dermal pitting I didn't see arrive.
I've never known beauty as an assault
carry such danger; and it's all my fault.

89 – (*See Shakespeare's Sonnet 99*)
His breath's scent is violets, it comes that sweet
with each deeply insinuating kiss
and it's in his pigmentation – upbeat
palette, part-light makeup, part-hidden stress.
I see flowers in his face (I'd like to crush
roses into his body and demand
a reciprocally sensual sex-rush)
and in the afterglow stamp on his hand.
There's round him an aura of white despair
the knowledge earth will fill his veins when dead
and the white flower I placed in his hair
like Billie Holiday, crumples on the bed.
I note these things, how flowers can't compare
with angles of his face, that profile, that stare.

•

90
Baby, the mirror's your worst commentary
it throws back at you city hours you waste
and the blackout pockets in your memory
programme the rest that's valueless as paste.
You need to go visit a cemetery
appreciate how little time you've got
to do anything, it's never easy
accepting we're compounded to slow rot.
Go educate yourself, you theme my book
without credentials, inequality's
my fault, acute obsession with your looks
and blaming you for no facility
to understand my writings, who could care
when we're atomized and no longer there?

91
You're so written in my memory
I'm sure your image will remain in death
as spooky virtual post-humanity
digitised atoms of integral self.
But for the moment you're in heart and mind
like 'The First Time Ever I Saw Your Face',
Roberta Flack's aching song to remind
how lovers fit an individual space.
There's days you're scrambled into disconnect,
but only partial, and come back full-on
as the troubled paradigm I re-select
to flood my cells. To me you're always on.
I don't need gifts from you, they're cheap and hurt
like stamping memories into street dirt.

●

92
All those great schemes, the monumental plans
I raised like a new office tower, the beach
I imagined beyond white horizons
where we'd continue always out of reach
after we died, but everything collapsed
like a shop raided by bailiffs for rent,
the tenants out for a shortfall relapsed
again, beaten by bricky thugs so bent
they're sub-contractual East End racketeers
sponsored by crack. Poets are poor but free
and we've both deconstructed bad careers,
me with two companies. You hold your own.
A leather wolf at night, you hunt alone.

93

Why don't I fuck off British poetry
and all its bores flat-footed as Ugg boots
go chase an energised vivacity
like US pioneers from Black Mountain roots?
I'm stuck with seeing myself in each word's
reinventive originality
my outlaw signature that's seen and heard
and noted for explosive imagery.
My subject never changes, comes up *you*,
there's no angle of love that's not been done,
it's just it's ours in every shade of blue
from Californian skies to a handgun.
We orbit the sun, it don't go away
just like my habit of writing this way.

.

94

I change in variants that make the change,
the pyramids were built by aliens,
ETs and zombies I've never thought strange –
they've rocket science and speed of light means.
We look behind us to see what's ahead,
our time's so brief every green light faces
down generational progress to a red
and new skyscrapers fill empty spaces.
We're both so hurried; a week's like a day,
a day an hour, an hour a nanosecond,
like most items wishing they'd always stay
together, we blow fuses and can't find
a resting point, like fins slicing the sky
through smoky cirrus. If you die I die.

95

I tell you, hun, all I write is lies,
the counterfactual dominates passion,
the whole thing's like Lee Harwood's 'As Your Eyes
Are Blue': sincerity's not in fashion.
So many accidents, randomised things
happen today, tomorrow and get lost,
pop stars, celebs, bankers, financiers, kings,
we scrape them off like black carbon on toast.
The present's all we've got, there's more for you
and less for me, the disproportion shows,
some desperation in the overview
like a rainy night when a red LED glows.
Our love's demanding from the first to last:
neither confesses their criminal past.

•

96

You're lowlife, which means gold dust in your veins,
my problem comes accepting you're human
not the time-slipped legendary remains
of Elvis Presley in a Coca Cola can.
It wasn't chance hitched us: we got it right
sometimes, contentious others, didn't care
about social networking every night
with clubby types, or that your blond-tipped hair
invited looks, or suggested a change
we wouldn't make – I mean the honesty
of being who you are, why rearrange
for hypocrites whose false identity
involves double lives, all those profiteers
corrupt and criminal as ministers.

97

Both personal and collective fears point
to dystopian meltdown, blow-out endgame,
to love I know will also disappoint
and it's the cash-king oligarchs to blame.
The moon's politicised as real estate
for space mining, Whitehall's a sick quango
of viral pundits: it's never too late
to start again and let sleaze merchants go.
We hike up a delicious interval
when worry of disease and death go blank
and London lingo reverts to tribal
and poets for a day loot every bank.
History's like flu, a viral pandemic
of lies to which bad reputations stick.

•

98 – (*See Shakespeare's Sonnet 105*)
Not marble, nor the glitzy trashy graves
of celebs will outlive this muscled rhyme,
but you'll shine brighter each time a word saves
the bite converting poetry into crime.
When war bombs a city into meltdown
and looters rock subsiding masonry,
you'll still survive as gossip in this town
compact in my resistant poetry.
You'll outlive death like that, and enmity
at being queer compounded in my lines
that seem to signpost a posterity
in world affairs where militant Czars shine.
You're like the summer hits lovers recall,
thinking back to a time they had it all.

99
The boredom of dead Sundays kills me most,
turning up photos of old glamour stars,
most of them hip declassified B-list
retrieved by poetry I write in bars.
Their fatal attraction, you've got it now,
movie-star features, pouty lips and eye,
and cool characteristics that somehow
do business class with champagne when you fly.
When you're in love, it seems most poetry
is written to describe the big event,
but always falls short, like the way I see
you throwing shapes in our colour moment.
We're too close to the present in our face,
to think of you I need an abstract space.

•

100
The new's updated at the speed of light,
despite reluctance to change, it's the brain
programmes space visitors in shuttled flight
from tomorrow into grey London rain.
Maybe 500 years ago we knew
each other, me as you and you as me,
the interchange like plotting green and blue
as variants of one reality.
I'd like to know if we were different
in looks and attitude and if same-sex
attraction pulled us into the moment
and if it's better no matter the hex
put on it, straight's always optimised norm,
and did we scandal-hit kick up a storm.

101

What's in the brain wiring pops chemically
that hasn't always, baby, been in you,
your merit as one-off bandit's to me
how we reinvent every moment new.
We try do what we do in this affair,
punter and rent and it's the usual game,
pretending we're the first, I muss your hair
and tell you lyingly we're just the same.
I'd like to think words reconstruct a face
like stem cells, or the surgeon's tuck resists
the lived-in creases that come to replace
the youthful image that we know exists
resistantly beneath the damage done
and couldn't care and live by going on.

•

102

My patron's loot helps sustain this affair,
Southampton's wealth, not a hedge funder's trash
or Arab black-gold glitzy billionaire
buying London towers with laundered cash.
I hope the stuff I write fulfils a need
in your perversity, helping lowlife
express itself, and that I've somehow freed
bits of you prohibited by your wife.
I know minds come together in the stars
before they meet, no matter rich or poor
and that this bandit poet cruising bars
gives you the gold found on a dirty floor.
PS I love you, it's our best secret
and kept submerged like the places we meet.

103

I'm like a singer flaky with stage fright
forgetting lines backstage: 'Take all of me',
and self- defeatingly can't get it right
as though black holes suck out my memory.
I never get on it; forget to say
what's unconditional, redress the wrong
impartially, then mess it up my way
pretending the apology's a song,
or eloquently argue a defence:
the real me's in my books and so are you
knowing I'm fabricating a pretence
you've heard so often as being untrue.
You'll hear in the silence what I feel
and if there's substance in it, if it's real.

•

104 – (*See Shakespeare's Sonnet 49*)
It's just a shot away, that ugly time
when my defects will outnumber good points
you liked in me, and you'll spit on my name
insisting every thing disappoints.
I'll watch the sparkle go out of your eyes
in cutting me, banging me up like scum,
and listening to your diatribe of lies
hear every mashed-up brain cell start to hum.
I try to prepare myself for the end,
boost my disillusioned dejected self
so lonely I'm on a desert island
dreaming how you were once my other half.
And before you were born, summers seemed dead
and now burn incandescently instead.

105 – *(See Shakespeare's Sonnet 113)*
Since leaving him I've grown doubly confused,
out of my mind with flashbacks, hurt, regret,
what's real, what's not, of course I stand accused
of forcing issues I'd rather forget.
Without him, there's no flower, bird or shape
assumes the easy curve of poetry
his input gives me. My work's give and take,
a visionary co-dependency.
The good and bad, there's no separation,
the perfect and deformed, he sees the two
as compatible, the crow and mountain
double for him in my fixated view.
It's down to him I get the juice I do
'But it's all over now, baby blue.'

•

106 – *(See Shakespeare's Sonnet 114)*
I'm just so full of you that flattery's
natural as truth. Language is such a lie
and we all do its sexy alchemy,
messing you up when I could pass you by.
You make bad times better, there's so many
need converting, you make the worst the best,
the monster in the back room showered in pee,
all the atrocities and all the rest.
I give him what he wants to hear and I
if I believe it, do the rest with drink,
as though my gift's distorted and I try
through alcohol to push us to the brink.
We've Tainted Love – the song – the poison too
is arsenic muddy grey or cobalt blue?

107

I'd rather be notorious, maligned,
down in the gutter; gold floats on black streams,
and *known* for it. Who'd have me realigned
from outlaw to mainstream pundits who cream
over redundant trash? A mean quango
shoot holes into my vulnerability,
reduce me to their limits, all they know
is drag me down, but my reality
is LSD to theirs; they're mostly straight
beefed-up machos despising queer culture
and arriving 100 years too late
to find me light years into the future.
They maintain power; it's the viral strain
compensating for all they can't attain.

•

108 – *(See Shakespeare's Sonnet 115)*
I always meant it, saying I love you,
but kept my distance, closer for the space
I opened, always hoping to renew
the nearness of you nothing can replace.
If I've been absent, too long on the road,
like Bob Dylan, then I always return
to you as singular focus and read
in the experience a chance to learn
new pathways, all that mileage in my blood
recycled to purity, mostly gone,
meaning a reinvention of my good
and back the chance to show you how I've shone.
You're the one rose in the wide universe
to whom I work bitty lines into verse.

109 – *(See Shakespeare's Sonnet 117)*
I've been avoiding you and it's too bad,
my silences, unexplained company,
my apparent ingratitude, it's sad
my rude boy attitude comes back to me.
I've dipped into the underworld again,
profiteers, racketeers, dodgy rent,
crowding my ruin on for selfish gain,
by now it's a sordid recurrent event.
You're right to feel neglected, part to blame
for my indifference, my drop into
the underground I trawl through without shame,
but hate's less operative than feeling blue.
It's weird I hurt you to accelerate
a hotter, sexier, abandoned date.

•

110 – *(See Shakespeare's Sonnet 116)*
I'd never disrupt harmony of minds
or put restraint on personal liberty
or try to alter all those tricky finds
that colour individuality.
What makes a person special's who they are
unmodified by anyone's control,
I mean inner resources, like a star
maintained and fixed by a personalised role.
Love transcends time; even if your blond hair's
a part of it so briefly, it's support
against knowledge of death and all those cares
that rip me up and you as an escort.
If I've got this all wrong, then nothing's right
the universe unplugged of all its light.

III – *(See Shakespeare's Sonnet 120)*
Even your insults are – sort of – reward,
I recreate the hurt to savour pain,
and if the fetish appears kinda weird
I like to do it all over again.
There's aspects of my cruelty shook you up
as violent run-ins; you came back at me
with saturated hate or made exit
from vicious reprisals, got out, got free.
If only we'd learnt caution from those hits
of animosity that struck at night
and making up the apology sits
awkwardly like words do after a fight.
We're at cross-purposes, but need to find
gateways from cruelty to being kind.

•

112
The news is out, our scandalous misfit
of personalities – you pity me!
And that's not love in our disturbed remit
of making out through inequality.
You're my whole world, of course I take the lot.
Good and bad, I'm dependent on your moods
and flip-side changes filtered cool and hot
and mostly on being misunderstood.
Another media target, I resist
telling my story, and get kicked so hard
I couldn't care if I'm on the hit list
I'd rather smoke a joint out in the yard.
It's only you I value: the world's dead
shattered by wars and crashed into the red.

113

I have this notion you're better than me
my broken-hearted love song says it all
although it's only introspectively
my blues like a blue from Farrow & Ball.
Let's try convince ourselves that we're for life
a single item like a single rose
even in separation you're my wife
the scabby Mister WH I chose.
Mostly the thought of separation kills,
absence would shatter, I can't take the thought
living for all the hedonistic thrills
being together means, although you're bought.
I call us two by undermining truth
me picking at the glace cherry – youth.

•

114

It's all a fantasy we can't be split
and help each other cope – where'd you get that
our juiced personalities never fit,
I suffer alone and you're a street rat?
We've got respect, but it's tempered by spite
and bitchy altercations that poison
our better days. We never get it right,
both in our separate ways causing friction.
I face you down in public and pretend
it's me that doesn't merit your cute look
or deserve more than pissing in the wind
can bring, but still you theme my wacky book.
But when we're up together, there's a glow
surrounds us like a blue floaty halo.

115

Add hate to everything I've lost and lose
now I'm rock bottom at my lowest point,
spit on me, beat me, whatever you choose
I've had so much nothing can disappoint.
And don't come crawling round pretending care
does anything but amplify ordeal,
it's like the rainy dawn at which I stare
after the storm, all brutally too real.
Don't delay the torment of leaving me,
successive threats, you turn the knife so slow
the agonized eventuality
of being ripped – I'd like it over now.
The pain of this submerges other grief
you've robbed me of being a common thief.

•

116

There's sweet reflective moments even slammed
against the wall, recreating a past
in which our best emotions studio-jammed,
I shouldn't see waste in what couldn't last.
I need to partner grief for those dead friends
absorbed anonymously into dark,
the absent ones who my writing attends
as though they're hidden in a leafy park.
A lifetime's deficit, we have our dead
like runaways who don't live anywhere,
I'm out of touch with them and need instead
to nurture hurt, be absolutely there
for all who've touched me, including you, friend,
sending orbital signals through my mind.

117 − *(See Shakespeare's Sonnet 94)*
The power to hurt, it's written in your face
checked by restraint, dissociated, blank,
the impassive occupy their own space
like your street-tough rival, runaway Frank.
This keeping closed expression like some do,
wins favours, but like charm it's mostly fake,
like politicians and sleazy Who's Who,
the frigid rictus done for its own sake.
Each summer flower's perfection for its cause
although unconsciously it lives to die
never contradicting entropy's laws,
its petals floating off into the sky.
Beauty gravitates to its opposite,
but even rotting lilies still smell sweet.

•

118 − *(See Shakespeare's Sonnet 110)*
Don't mess with destiny, you can't reverse
the bad I've broken thinking it was right,
I've lived on little means, it could be worse
my public following, I wear it light.
I'm a brand like the Rolling Stones, Shakespeare,
confined by what's expected and subdued
by working in those limits, I've the fear
the energies I've used can't be renewed.
I try to modify, look for pathways
of self-help, bitter that I can't correct
unmended damage in my broken days
or accept how this poison can infect.
Don't pity me, although the least kindness
will somehow alleviate my distress.

119 – (*See Shakespeare's Sonnet 60*)
Time's like a wave breaking over the shore
irreversible momentum in the cells.
Nothing that kicks in now or went before
means anything – I tell you it's fuck all.
We're born, self-identified, pushed into
a system peaking at maturity
DNA error working like voodoo
to smash expectations of longevity.
Beauty in youth's inimitably great
and for a time seems permanent, who'd think
it's over so fast, a transient state
so quickly lived-in and ruined by drink?
I come back to the hope my poems last
documenting bits of your damaged past.

•

120
Defaced by time, there's no option in this,
expensive looks disintegrate, you've seen
it in yourself and others what you miss
and can't reinvent, the glamour you've been.
I've seen the ocean rip into the land
its shattering force smashing all frontiers
and later on reversed the blazing sand
appear as insurmountable barrier.
It's this crazy exchange repeats patterns
I can't correct, decay in everyone

including me and him, the slow returns
of believing this man's the only one.
I'd rather he was dead than had to die,
gone like a plane winging it through the sky.

121

A sugar daddy tries to relive youth
by seeing in his bit of trade the juice
he's lost, knowing the spooked, unfocused truth
is that it's over, Viagra his choice.
Whatever life gives, it also takes back,
beauty, wealth, talent or this poet's gift
so that abundance also describes lack
and ageing's not solved by a quick face-lift.
I feed into your vibrant energies
as a quick sustained fix, and live
on those resources, not on memories
of Heaven, Club Magenta, a dance groove.
I want the best for you; it's good for me
to see you out and living dangerously.

•

122 – *(See Shakespeare's Sonnet 110)*
It's true my reputation follows me,
my notoriety, I've sold out cheap,
faked contracts, offended most company,
dipped in the Thames Pool, where black water's deep
and deeper still. Manipulating truth
I've learned a deviant aspect boots-up
exhausted debilitated impetus
like a pathway opened by a new app.
I've done the lot, and, baby, there's no end
to what I'd do to singularize your love,
I've tried it all; you're always on my mind
as friend, the only one I'd have survive.
So make me welcome, need me like your breath,
and so intensely I lose fear of death.

123

The morning after – booze tastes like poison
and won't compensate for the tears that flood
confusion in my nerves, I never win,
the loser cooks distress in toxic blood.
The wrong I've done I always thought was good
and not reactive accumulative error
too distracted to read oppressive mood
as what it was to you acute terror.
Reflective dawns, shaken awake, I view
good and bad interactively, they feed
on each other vicious like me and you
and evil's better when it's met by need.
I learn my lessons messing with your mind
twisting your thoughts and hurting to be kind.

•

124 – (*See Shakespeare's Sonnet 118*)
No satisfaction in feeding my face
my palate needs a Heston Blumenthal,
disease working to occupy a space
most diets kill by high cholesterol.
I'm full of you, your sweetness and your rough,
and neither satisfy – the bitter's best
and illnesses you carry as street tough
infect me, but I hardly ever test.
Me needing you, your sickness is the cure
correcting expectations of the worst
pandemics, knowing it's in your nature
to heal me by disease, I'm not the first.
You've stitched me up; you're like a Class A drug
I should have left in bottom of the bag.

125

My fall's sensationally mediatized
and as the countermeasure I'm alone
and throwing desperate shapes, I realise
this time I've blown it and I'm too far gone
to repair damage done: you hear me now,
other men's friends and assets, tax-free wealth
seem enviable after this hammered blow
threatening to put me into mental health.
It's just, the thought of you sustains the hope
of a remake – like waiting for the dawn's
pomegranate light still half-stunned from dope
and hearing birdsong activate the lawn.
You're gold in my veins and they flood with light
making every molecule appear bright.

•

126

You're far too good for me and free to go,
it's unconditional, the bond we share,
you're liberated in this deal, you know;
a sugar daddy offers to be fair.
I've no patent on you, kept pretty-boy,
or the bent trust we maintain at a cost,
I see you as unmanageable toy,
if I'm the loser you're equally lost.
It's all confused, the things we did and said,
you undervalued your worth on the street,
sold yourself cheap and now you're in the red
but fill a punter's frozen veins with heat.
I dreamed you'd never leave me – what a dream,
like finding your drowned body in a stream.

127

Those lips I'd shaped into a glossy pout
as substitute for Will spit sneering hate,
despite appeasements she shouts 'Just get out,
go back to him, your crawling comes too late.'
But when she softens, graduates to sweet,
I feel a corresponding change in me
a psychic wake-up that we had to meet
the three of us as complex destiny.
But when she changes tone, 'It's him, not you,
that money-guzzler I've come to resent,
how can I tolerate your point of view
that there's redeemable qualities in rent?'
and tries to make-up – I resist her kiss,
storm back to Southwark and give it a miss.

•

128 – (See Shakespesre's Sonnet 128)

It's not the guitar, it's your fluent hand
and rapid finger-picking achieves sound
the riffy licks my senses understand
generically pulled from the underground.
Mostly I envy festival front-lines
the ones who look directly in our eyes
and get off when your virtuoso shines
and grab you, under rainy English skies.
Everything changes with the volume up
and open-tuning, you're so iconized,
fans start to lose it and the crowd lets rip,
new inclusions leaving them surprised.
I'd like to find you in that churning mass
of random bodies and ignite a kiss.

129
In love we don't do morals or offend
by lack of conscience, we do our own thing
and if you pick up my bad ways pretend
they're really yours – partners share everything.
You sleep around, betray me, I'm to blame
for self-debasement, lack of self-respect,
and even though I get above my shame
good aspects of me fall into neglect.
If you're my prize it comes at a rough cost
of lowering, I've lost my pride to you
and all the others, they would fill a list
that colours my heart fifty shades of blue.
You're worth the lot – my guilt's a twisted trust
pushed to subservient edges of lust.

•

130
You check my nearness for identity,
I'm always someone else, you're never clear,
the poet's schizoid personality
transmits 'I'm so touched by your presence dear'.
It's always tricky being a cool ace,
prime mover in my numerology
where one and zero meet in the same space
though neither colours as a primary.
If my starting point's Number One, I move
immodestly to leaving you behind,
though it's you, honey, who sweetens my groove
and switches a light bulb on in my mind.
We're both Will, same name, if you're on the game
writing up your underground wins me fame.

131 – (*See Shakespeare's Sonnet 135*)
You've got your Will, try Billy for a change,
in this threesome your bitchy appetite
wants all of me, something I rearrange
by giving you the occasional night.
You won't accept the bargain as it sucks
nor stabilise my desperate sleeping around,
nor see me sparkle, how it's my shine fucks
with the inventory of trade I've lost and found.
The river's flooded with turbulent rain
and keeps on pushing frontiers in its rip
and if you had the savvy to turn pain
to resources I wouldn't get your lip.
Try generosity: see loss as gain,
the endless recycle comes round again.

•

132 – (*See Shakespeare's Sonnet 143*)
A woman, and her child's a runaway
to the capital's dark underbelly,
she leaves the lot to chase him every day
thinking only of his recovery
from vice and its potentialities.
He knows he's tracked and almost turns around
his mind gravitating to memories
of better moments when mum turned up kind.
And we're no different pursuer/pursued,
the roles exchanged so often neither knows
who's in the lead and who is being used,
who's kind, and if we'll come to blows.
Let's reconnect, rehabilitate care
to my bottomless, crying-out despair.

133

So now it emerges that he's fucked you too,
and that's my optimal focus, the part
of him that elusively lives in you
there in the red ballroom inside your heart.
You're stuck together now like super glue,
you by possessiveness, and he's so kind,
at least the aspects of him that I knew,
you're sure to mess his reconstructed mind,
the one I taught to write, you're a fag-hag
using your body like a walk-up whore.
Despite Will's propensity to do drag,
he's left me for the red light on your floor.
I've lost him, now you've got the two of us
as a devious promiscuous bonus.

•

134 – (*See Shakespeare's Sonnet 133*)
You've smashed us up; I'm broken and alone,
your scheming intervention's left me wrecked,
the mental torment's like a slow poison;
he's traumatised in ways that can't be checked.
You've done for me and my integrity
and set him back like a recidivist
and now we're all warring with enmity
all of us wishing we didn't exist,
and there's no resolution to free fall,
I want him, either way; with you or me
and desperately, there's no way at all
I'll give him up to your duplicity.
It's touch and go – I'd cut your heart in three
and of course divide it unequally.

135 – (*See Shakespeare's Sonnet 134*)
I give it all away and liberally
floaty promises, a plague pandemic
sweating off walls, your inconsistency
having you love and hate – I think you're sick
in oscillating with violent mood swings
between the two, while I break all the laws
abusing trust and all those little things
I misuse, swiping you with lion's paws.
I've used your kindness, stating mine's the same,
sworn inseparable togetherness
to do the opposite, bleeding your name
with all the fake in my coarse bitterness.
I've lied to you and to myself no end
to driving both us losers round the bend.

•

136
I've made a cult of wrong and partnered hate
and secretly get deeper into vice,
I mean, the two of us, we're always late
to correct errors – like braking on ice.
You use your lips for trade, they're glossy red,
signalling fatal attraction and rent
well practiced in the art of giving head
robbing the punter to confirm you're bent.
I love you all the same: you importune
with twinkling eyes the way I look at you
as though the moment's always opportune
to go get it, of course it's nothing new.
You try to hide it, but what I project
are the same motives you try to reject.

137

You rule me with your mad obdurate power,
I've no defences against your control,
you fist me open like smashing a flower
and there's no brightness in this ruthless deal.
Your mastery of evil leaves me numb,
manipulation proves a second art,
and like most losers I'm under your thumb,
I try to make your bad good in my heart.
You found my chronic masochistic bias
and how it turns me on, treated like shit
by your abhorrent surges of abuse
I take because the likeness seems to fit.
There's no accounting for the way we twist
relations, like veins knotted in a wrist.

•

138 – (*See Shakespeare's Sonnet 147*)

My love's incurable, the more you hurt
the more I relish it, like a disease
I've turned perversely into a comfort
accepting the pain like it's there to please.
I've lost all reason, like doing a drug
that wrecks me but fulfils a need,
knowing desire is death – it's such a drag
the doctor's prescription isn't for speed.
I'm past all cure and really couldn't care
and so distraught I think I'm losing it,
out of my mind with a psychotic stare,
convulsions, seizures or a mini-fit.
I got it wrong – I saw it in your face
you're really black as no-colour deep space.

139
Sometimes libido cools a day or two,
inaction fires-up the need for more,
in a brothel there's no breaking taboo,
there's a harem of toughs behind the door.
Or if it's women there'll be a black stud
who pimps and lords it over all with size
grooming propensities for every mood
with curvier demands the final prize.
The danger's that you get an STD
from Tudor hygiene, Emilia's focus
for every strain of resistant disease,
but I don't care, I'd rather as bonus
ride her bare back, precaution last resort
I use with Will as agency escort.

•

140 – (*See Shakespeare's Sonnet 153*)
The young man (you) curls up and goes to sleep
in a valley: a teen girl happens on
your body, it's a cameo she'll keep,
the denimed outline of your erection
she coaxes into action, couldn't care
about the consequences, urgency
increasing danger and licentious dare,
she's caught up in orgasmic ecstasy.
I've got transmissible disease, we're three
in this contention, no inhibitions
but piling on sexual velocity;
the clinic advised me take precautions,
but you're my cure – how can we ever stop,
three of us suspended over the drop.

141 – (*See Shakespeare's Sonnet 130*)
Emilia's eyes don't sparkle like sunshine,
there's redder brands of lipstick – Ruby Woo,
than her dull choice, her blueblack hair lacks shine,
she's only B-cup and I'm telling you
she's got no purchase on a hot red rose
applying blusher – I'm a makeup freak;
the perfume she wears lacks a Chanel nose
and doesn't get upgraded for a week.
I criticise her speech, nasal cockney,
and have no right, I'm into girl singers,
and when she walks the objective's money
with glitzy paste rainbowed on stashed fingers.
And yet she's got it, wow factor, street cred,
and clubbing Saturdays turns every head.

•

142 – (*See Shakespeare's Sonnet 141*)
Imagination's my reality;
I see your altered state as who you are
like the distorted visual frames I see
in mirrored reflections thrown off the bar.
Love's chemistry hallucinates the true,
if there's one way of seeing I don't know
why all these multi-variants of you
come up as clones with an aura's rainbow.
And yet my vision's shot with tears and dread
and fractured splinters of defiant trust,
it's all confusion, seeing blue as red
like a city sun sighting through puffed mist.
I'm blind to all your faults, the lawless side
observed as something that you needn't hide.

143
Don't call on me to justify your wrongs
the ratty mistrust that you lay on me
throwing vicious looks and those verbal stings
that slash my art and sensibility.
You boast of conquests, they're anonymous,
pin hotties with your eyes and couldn't care
picking up in front of me vacuous
street-trash in dirty denim with waved hair.
I'd let it go, I've done the same myself,
confining the world to a pretty face
and hurting someone by the obvious stealth
I take in invading a rival's space.
Don't do it to me, I can't stand the pain
that kills me over and over again.

•

144
Try work with wisdom, not just cruelty,
breaking me with systematic disdain,
words are my one defence, the weaponry
I use in poetry to offset pain.
Better for me to push your intellect
to wider frontiers, I hang on your lip
like someone dying hoping to select
a super drug, but all you do is strip
me of defences, driving me half mad
hysterically saying things I regret
so I up my capacity for bad.
You provoke the worst in me, you're so sly
putting me down, but looking in my eye.

145

The man in black who condescends to look
contemptuously on the comfort zone
I need, despising my lyrical hooks,
buried my heart, left me strung out alone.
His sad eyes grey like light-polluted sun
pushing through low cloud over the East End
are moody like they don't mean what they've done
or starlight too distant to ever find.
It's crazy that I play at being dead
to win attention, it's a subtle game
gone wrong, it's pity that I want instead
and part of your twistedness needs the same.
Beauty is black, not by pigment, but right,
and exemplifies the flip-side of light.

•

146 – *(See Shakespeare's Sonnet 127)*

Black's back in fashion, was it ever out
to men in dandified black, it's acute
tempo lends gravity – black skin proves it,
a no-colour tone that's unisex cute.
We don't know what's natural, makeup obscures,
at the same time excites, Emilia
dyes her hair black, the blackest of allures,
I keep the brand as memorabilia.
When her quizzical eyes narrow they're black
with vehement vengeance – they want me dead
and in their focus proposition lack
of notice if it's me inside her bed.
It's when they're saddest they're most beautiful,
pulling attention like a black canal.

147
You use your beauty as a selling-point
promiscuous weaponry that makes you cruel,
knowing that, inhaling your whiffy joint,
I see you blaze like an amazing jewel.
Others don't see your looks the way I do
as paramount to inciting desire,
but think it's an obsession needing you
to be revised when the next one appears.
Of course it's fetishistic that you're black
as preference, a very personal choice
triggering hot gossip behind my back,
I'm into weird associative vice.
The slander proceeds from the curious things
I buy you, like a fist of stolen rings.

•

148 – (*See Shakespeare's Sonnet 141*)
It's not the way you look breaks me apart,
or wanting you because you're criticized,
I wear you like a ruby in my heart
no matter how intensely you're despised.
You're often rough as Will; I go for trade,
your voice is common and you're cultureless,
but that's the attraction, as I'm afraid
of class, and go by instinct more or less.
I wouldn't recommend you to a friend,
you're an odd choice in your appeal to me,
and even though our love affair will end
I'm hooked insatiably on your beauty.
I've got the plague from you and would again
as a comforting reassuring pain.

149 – *(See Shakespeare's Sonnet 149)*
You can't accuse me of indifference,
I go against the grain to be with you,
defy the system, it never makes sense,
self-destruct poets do just what they do.
Friends hate me and I hate their hypocrisy
and dislike your sycophantic groupies,
but we work out our sexual jealousy
accelerating new intensities.
Self-pride, the strain infects my character,
having me downgrade what others admire
about your personality and war
with how your eyes transmit constant desire.
Hate me and love me, don't I know your kind
deliriously screwing up my mind.

•

150 – *(See Shakespeare's Sonnet 141)*
Blinded by love I never see you right,
only idealised, and I've lost track
of who you are, lack clarity of sight –
I'm not even sure if you're white or black?
I come back to your eyes that polarise
a room by sexual inference and seem
to pull men in before they realise
like me they're sucked into a dangerous dream.
I'm not special, but more a public space
in the wide world that's used by everyone
who fucks you, thinking they're first in that place,
their misjudgement like mine obscured by fun.
I've got it wrong so often, just can't learn
I'm a repeat loser at every turn.

151 – (*See Shakespeare's Sonnet 138*)
I don't believe your lies; you sleep around,
your reassurances don't mean a thing,
I'm not incredulous; I know you've found
sexual variants in each casual fling.
I'm too old for you, Will's my preference,
although I act young like the Rolling Stones,
their social defiance my reference
point: we're both liars with deceiving tones
suppressing truth for its alternative,
a double life as a kind of fake gold,
I know how you're selling sex to survive
and you've intuited I'm really old.
We flatter each other by telling lies
and neither feels need to avert their eyes.

•

152 – (*See Shakespeare's Sonnet 129*)
No shame wasted on activating lust
or sexual prejudice can take away
its savage pleasures and abandoned trust,
rude ecstasies of being straight or gay,
and when it's over there's irrational guilt
at hurting, using, abusing someone,
because like road rage we're mad in pursuit
and orgasm's explosive as a gun.
We lose all inhibitions in the act
of coming, often it's a fantasy
we're riding, surfing channels to select
a mental image as reality.
We've all experienced it, conflicting thrills,
hoping it pleasures as much as it kills.

153 – *(See Shakespeare's Sonnet 144)*
Two opposites comfort and despair,
like a binary star preoccupy;
one's Will, who occupies the highest star,
the other's a slut who would have me die
the hardest self-destructive way, destroy
my civil partnership, abuse my Will,
shatter my creativity, employ
undercurrents of propulsive evil
to hammer him as wrong, establish guilt
because we love each other, who is she
to corner my friend, whip him with a belt
and accuse him of abnormality?
But we'll subvert her, call her common shit
and make the song into a massive hit.

•

154
Poor love, the epicentre of my life,
don't take the denigration heaped on you
by business suits who mortgaged to a wife
lack all originality and view
our lives as error, want to see you dead
for attitude and same-sex, have you rot
lower than trash on a verminous bed,
as though your kindness has deserved the lot.
Trust in your soul to compensate for loss
of the material world, there's inner gold
stored in the nerves, unlike a banker's dross,
and better dead you're safe from growing old.
So make of death a party in the sky,
there's never a right time or place to die.

Jeremy Reed has been for decades Britain's most dynamic, adventurous, and controversial poet. He has published over 40 books of poetry, fiction and non-fiction, winning prestigious literary prizes like the Somerset Maugham Award, and was on his coming to live in London in the 1980s patronised by the artist Francis Bacon. His biggest fans are JG Ballard, Pete Doherty and Björk who has called his work 'the most beautiful, outrageously brilliant poetry in the world.' Jeremy writes about every subject that British poetry considers taboo: glamour, pop, rock, sci-fi, cyber, mutant, gay, drugs, neuroscientific, the disaffected and outlawed, and the fizzy big city chemistry of the London in which he lives and creates.

•

EYEWEAR PUBLISHING